{ THIS FULL *green* HOUR }

THIS **FULL** *green* HOUR

AN ANTHOLOGY
BY THE ONE O'CLOCK POETS

GUILLERMO CASTRO

AMY LEMMON

KATRINKA MOORE

JOAN LAURI POOLE

ELIZABETH POREBA

SARAH STERN

Published by Sonopo Press
Copyright © 2008 by the One O'Clock Poets:
    Guillermo Castro, Amy Lemmon, Katrinka Moore, Joan Lauri Poole,
    Elizabeth Poreba, Sarah Stern
ISBN: 978-0-6152-1589-1
Cover Photograph/Art: Guillermo Castro. Used by permission.
Cover/Interior design: Tracey Munz Cataldo.
Text composition: Tracey Munz Cataldo, Barbara Sabella

Text set in Baskerville.
Printed in the United States of America.

987654321

First Edition

THE LIFE
by Helen Ruth Freeman

What is left is memory,
the gulped swallow of desire,
the anecdotal love
that over the years
weaves tapestries of living,
the feel of learning:
to seek and overreach,
to return to dross,
to earth and sky,
to everyone.

In memory of our dear friend and colleague
Helen Ruth, in whose home we first met

CONTENTS

INTRODUCTION

by Sarah Stern with interruptions

At one of our recent meetings, we were trying to pinpoint when the One O'Clock Poets first met. Nobody could say exactly, although it was agreed upon that it was sometime shortly after 9/11, possibly January or February of the following year. The amazing thing about this discussion was that nobody had to say, "We met on February 15, 2002." Nobody had to be definitive. Everybody said something, and then we moved on. In the more than six years we have been meeting, there has never been complete consensus about anything—not poetry, not life, not even a single comma.

> GUILLERMO: *Ladies, maybe we should talk about Why We Call Ourselves The One O'Clock Poets: Once a month, usually on a Sunday at two o'clock in the afternoon, the group meets. And one hour before the appointed time you can count on similar scenes of quasi-slapstick simultaneously unfolding as the poets scramble to finish— or as close to finishing as possible—the Poem they'll be soon sharing with each other. Never like now do the digits on the various time-keeping devices seem more vicious and impatient. Finally, we're out the door, blowing kisses to our amused significant others while still getting dressed, which will surely cause us to take a serious tumble down the stairs (yet that fall could spark new ideas!). After all, the task of revising is hardly over, if it ever really is. On the way to the workshop, in our preferred mode of transportation—car, train, jetpack—you will find us, pen or pencil in hand, feverishly crossing out words or entire lines, scrawling new ones, or using the reverse of the page to write a complete new work, oblivious to the world we work so hard to disrobe. I could tell you more, but frankly, I've got to finish my poem first.*

Yet when we meet something happens to all of us. It can only be expressed as letting go—meaning letting go of our egos— meaning being honest, respectful—democratic in the noblest sense of the word.

After we gather at Elizabeth's or Katrinka's or Joan's place, or as we did in the first few years, at Helen Ruth Freeman's apartment, we schmooze a bit, then someone says—the host, or someone else eager to get to the work at hand—"let's start." With that, we begin to pass around our work. First, the author reads a poem, and then the person to the author's right reads it again so that the author gets to hear it, too.

> JOAN: *I first learned this technique from Galway Kinnell— the importance of hearing your words coming from someone else's mouth. Where the reader fumbles may be the worst or the best part of the poem, but hearing another person saying the words is always jarring and often shows you where your poem is alive or dying.*

As the discussion begins, the author listens without commenting. We adhere to the workshop convention of holding authors' responses until the end of the discussion of their work. A poet responds with questions, responds to the readers' questions, or says nothing at all except "Thanks."

Once the discussion begins, what matters is what's on the page— nothing else. Looking solely at the poem—the subject matter, the physical form, the sounds, the line breaks, the white space created—we all become navigators in a new world. As navigators, we look at what is pulling us in one direction, what's repelling us, and what's sending us in a direction where we may or may not want to go. Ultimately, we get to what's blinding us and what's making us see something we never saw before.

> AMY: *For me, being in the group has provided the impetus (and the deadline) necessary to bring poems out of my notebook, or even my head, and onto a printed page. I know for a fact that many of the poems I've been able to produce would not have happened without the group, or would at least have come out differently (and probably not as well).*

A longtime mentor, looking at a manuscript of my poems, noted a substantial change in my work from a previous version. When I mentioned that I had been working on the newer poems with my group, she said, "Ah. You've been writing for your best readers."

Our discussions may center on one line, the poem's overall impact, one word, the title, or even the placement of a period—such minutiae as poets are known to fixate on. There are usually conflicting thoughts about what works, and there is never pressure to find one overriding way to "fix" the poem. The poet listens and in some magical way may take something away that is crucial to the poem. The poem may come back again revised, may sit for a while and take shelter, or may be sent out for publication.

ELIZABETH: *Or it may, in my case at least, never see the light of day again. I've progressed to the point where I can bring in real clunkers, either to confirm my own diagnosis—the group can do this in a very gentle way—or to get help ferreting out the one organ that is keeping the beast alive. I know the group believes in me enough to understand that one disastrous poem is not a disaster, and might even be a sign of growth.*

Once the poem comes to the workshop it's almost as though it's given a life, it comes out into the open, like a foal adjusting to its new legs.

JOAN: *Over time, I've noticed how alert we have become to one another's quirks and tics, but such awareness must be handled deftly. How do we encourage each other to remain loyal to the unique character of our work and at the same time nudge each other outward into the field of a new kind of poem?*

As we read the poems, a word triggers associations in each member of the group that we might not have experienced outside the group. You may think we'd start to sound like each other, but in fact we are all quite different in the way we put words on paper, in our sensibilities, and in what moves us. It's almost as if our voices become clearer and more distinct because we are able to sound off against each other. We are all in this together, searching for meaning and connection, struggling with the limitations of language itself.

> KATRINKA: *Yes, we're searching—together—but not for the same meanings. Each poet has her or his own themes—passions, obsessions—to follow. Our influence on one another is slant, not precise. I was inspired by the many different shapes of my colleagues' poems to experiment in visual poetry, which has taken my work in a new direction. And I think we've all been affected by the diversity of interests. In any given meeting we may learn about an arcane detail of biblical history, astrophysics, the term* midrash, *or the pronunciation of a certain Spanish word around the world.*

When the group ends, we usually walk out together; some go uptown, some downtown, to Brooklyn, the Bronx, Queens, Westchester—even to Utah. The poems have been shaped by our way of working. They are richer and more grounded, and because of these exchanges we ourselves are more profoundly human. This collection is a small testament to that experience.

THE SKY REMINDED *me*

AZZURRO

The sky reminded me today
of Italy,
except—no cupids.

Sometimes you want to be
something else—
the way the small black birds
sit at the ends
of the bare branches
pretending to be leaves.

As I stared at the clouds,
the desire came over me
to study Italian.
Una bella donna,
una ragazza dolce,
molti uomini—
all those vowels.

In Japan, the Shinkansen
bullet train
shot by the emerald rice fields'
immortal glistening.

And in Hiroshima, old and young
rode English racers—
la bicicletta,
un bosco oscuro.
It was a comfort—
their bike lights on in the dark.

Have you thought much
about the *bit*
in *ambition*—
the bit that wounds
and the bit that reins
wildness in?

Or about the words themselves
deserving homage—
submissive prisms
through which light unbraids itself
into colors
just passing through.

He pulled the curtain against the sun
that beat into our living room

as if it had pressed closer
and sworn an end to winter.

Finally light,
followed by too much

and the shutting out of what
we thought we could never have enough.

I languished in the heat.
He stood and with a sweep

shut out summer's greens.
Too hot to speak.

Pine planks swelled
with the weight of past rains.

The ice in our glasses stirred
and forgot its solid state.

Nothing is as strong as that sun.
A marriage melted to an afternoon.

CLEAR NIGHT OUTSIDE RITE-AID WITH JUPITER OVERHEAD

I love that moment before it becomes
in little Leah's words
"really really really dark,"
and the sky turns slightly purplish
blue, when streetlights
that have stood sentinel
for years as I walked by
in my full spectrum of moods
begin coming on.
If then I cast my eyes down the wide avenues
and across the slim side streets—
space rising between the highest buildings,
as palpable for now
as the skyscrapers themselves—
I find myself caught for an instant
between the flesh and emptiness,
the cozy and the stark.

MONDAY AUBADE

As I open my eyes the long spine shifts
before me to accommodate the bed's
straight surface, and suddenly I'm lost
in male odalisque, the much-loved back
a visible yawn, freckled and luxuriant.

Later, I stand with a dozen strangers
close enough to kiss. Instead, we avoid
each other's eyes for the eternal six blocks
from Penn Station to 28th Street.
Each detail of our situation begs
and yet forbids intimacy—the casual touch,
smells of perfume and shampoo,
the stray sneeze and perfunctory blessing.
Each with our mussed exigencies,
we blend in a rough subterranean dance
then struggle to burst up and out,
stagger up the stairs to the natural light
of morning as the day composes itself,
face by blessèd face.

A line on the lake, one side in shadow,
the other in light.   Four ducks swim
one after the other—see their backs glow—
to the line on the lake, to the side in shadow.

A rowboat drifts, the birds shift to a row.
As sun hits the prow, the fowl reach the rim,
cross the line on the lake, enter the shadow.
The other's in light. Boat, ducks, whim.

FOUR-HUNDRED MILLION LIGHT-YEARS AWAY

two black holes draw closer together
in a dance. Remarkable. They'll collide
in another one-hundred million years.

Waves will race across the universe,
touching everything they pass, briefly
warping space, making planets pulse,

satellites jiggle. Navigational
equipment will wobble. How small we are
in our linear world. Hopeful too

that some one will notice the pictures
on the walls have tilted,
that the moon is shivering.

The newspaper had a picture,
two Rorschach splats of light,
oranges, reds, and purples making

their way toward each other,
as Adam and God are,
index fingers extended.

I'm really sorry for what happened to you, Darling.
There might be blood on your hands
Yet you move them so fast over the keyboard
You'll be rid of it in about seventeen minutes.
And all the things at one point I was saving to tell you
—only through this kingdom of words—
Are forgotten now. In the meantime use this rag please
To wipe the computer keys. Let's see what kind of poem
The cleaning motion will produce: *jkjhvl;knb*.
Try one more time: *flnml;hgfoijk*.
For better results use your fingertips. Also,
There are spiders —your fingers again?—
Shadowboxing everywhere. What sort of enormous
Ocean made of some indescribable material
Would freeze its waves in the shape of this catatonic
Cathedral between us? Hard to tell. And that day
You really scared me as we stood in the rain,
Both muted by the demon tumbling inside
Your head and throat. But tonight
May your household in Brooklyn sleep in peace
While in your open, clean palms
You cradle your poem, your new poem.

OFTEN **THE**
CONCEPT
comes without the WORD

Either from the center or to
the center. Start by the creek
deep in the hemlocks, take
the sun-spilled path. Or
walk from the road
through ghost trees
hardwoods
felled
making
way for thorns
catching at you
holding you, brambles
so thick you've got to stomp
a path in, arms raised above
fierce black raspberries. To or from.

A GOOD WORD LIKE THAT

I do get it.
Listen, I've already adopted some precious sounds

For a flagless land of the mind I not only call
The Mother but also the Daughter;

And I am torn between the two
In a distant field
Somewhere amid perky words
As a lessee of American English—

And I'm ready to discharge my guns
On some savage minutemen at the checkpoint.

I take them as they come, words, sometimes one by one,
Sometimes as a pack, strays mooching
About the muy mucho dangerous borders.

Clearly they're not pretty spaniels
Under all that clouding trouble called the sky.

Meanwhile el brain en Español
Sits there wagging its spinal cord in a show of pure,
Fetching want

I shall resist: I don't ever ask of it
For an equivalent on any given word in English
Volleyed our way.

Yet watching this young girl in a movie
Translate into Spanish for her mom
I hear "Get it?" interpreted as "¿Entiende?"

Of course! To be more like that girl
And think of a good word like that. Listen—

I'm singing to my precious sounds, my children,
Spanglish, Espanglés and Englishñol.

TO PREPARE FOR PRAYER,

First, acknowledge.
acknowledged
that's just my face

But I did yesterday—
and still don't know—
in the black window.

Ack—   ack—
—know   —no
nothing where granite

—now
ledge here—
lintels were

And beyond the edge
from her bed
strewn that month

that view—
of the little hill
with daffodils.

SALUTATIONS TO LORCA

I leave the office and boy—the day is done, dark and wet.
It's not a bad life, mind you, this patch of universe
At the bottom of some terrifying ocean.
Here I am, timid and devoured by fog.
All these surrounding buildings like fantastic teeth!
Something in a raggedy shape rises from the clock tower.
What are my plans for the revolution today? Oh yeah, break all
Windows and release their tea-colored silence.
Once again in my thoughts, Federico—hi there.
My salty thoughts I lick and try to keep clean.
But with every step I tiptoe, five years fly by.

FIFTH GRADERS' QUESTIONS TO A POET

for Willie

What do you do if you get stuck?
Are you poor, so-so, or rich?
How did you become a poet?

Does poetry ever upset you?
Do you wish to be anything else?
Did you ever have other dreams?

Are you friends with other poets?
Did you like poetry when you were a kid?
How old are you?

What do you write about?
Do you have different feelings about your poems than others do?
Did you ever imagine you would be this when you were little?

If you weren't a poet what would you be?
Do you like reading?
Does it help you write the poems?

Does it take you a long time
to write one poem or a little time
to write lots of poems?

Do you like being asked questions?
Where do you get your ideas?
Do you write about yourself?

What do you write with a pen or a pencil?
What do you do when you're not writing poems?

SHEER

As in April the flower called twinleaf
folds to shoulder its straight stem
for as long as the weather holds,
perfect from leaf base to flower,
petals clenched to pearls held tight
above the jetsam of spring floods—

so love, slight, a sheer thing,
but absolute, from outside
the mind or time, a strand
pulled from the fleece of an invisible beast,
saves for no good reason
even if forgotten, denied, regretted
just because of something
underneath, a ground swell.

{ THE WORD *itself* }

THE ZAMBONI DRIVER

Since I was seven I've wanted to drive
the Zamboni onto the emptied rink
then methodically rid the ice of all
scratches until it gleams. After the war

he went back to his village, his own room.
Everything in the house was the same, even
the nail where now a crucifix hangs.

Second best would be skating out first
after he unlocked the white door. Parents
never really know their children. I'd make
deep cuts, rounding the bend before the rest.

GUILLOTINE POEM

Cut it out.
You could die like this!

The day manages to stick
To your tongue.
Wicked couples divorce
And ask for a refund.

Canine-like and shivering
Spread on your lover's bed.
You're trying to compose a poem.
Treat yourself right, hombre—(a)void the TV.

Scramble the rare text
From the local bookstore
After a walk through fiendish weather.

Once again you paw that yap-yap on the page
Which soon enough will turn
Into an inconsolable, dull friend.

Say, "The day feels as subtle as a guillotine."
Your name even almost spells it.

KARYOTYPE

<table>
<tr><td>What would</td><td>it look like,</td></tr>
<tr><td>I wondered,</td><td>this map</td></tr>
<tr><td>of gene particles,</td><td>counted</td></tr>
<tr><td>and crossed?</td><td>As we waited</td></tr>
<tr><td>I imagined</td><td>a tidy grid</td></tr>
<tr><td>of lines</td><td>and numbers,</td></tr>
<tr><td>stark spirals</td><td>in red-green-blue,</td></tr>
<tr><td>anything but</td><td>these tiny worms</td></tr>
<tr><td>photographed,</td><td>magnified, and ordered</td></tr>
<tr><td>in pairs except</td><td>for the infamous</td></tr>
<tr><td>twenty-first:</td><td>the error,</td></tr>
<tr><td>the glitch,</td><td>the wrench</td></tr>
<tr><td>in your infant</td><td>clockwork. Striped</td></tr>
<tr><td>and annelidic,</td><td>the chromosomes</td></tr>
<tr><td>weren't even</td><td>yours, just</td></tr>
<tr><td>a picture</td><td>of someone</td></tr>
<tr><td>else's, someone</td><td>else's child</td></tr>
<tr><td>who also had</td><td>too much,</td></tr>
<tr><td>too many worms.</td><td>I picture</td></tr>
<tr><td>the other parents</td><td>seeing these</td></tr>
<tr><td>squirming</td><td>for the first time   squinting hard</td></tr>
<tr><td>like we do now.</td><td>You're here.</td></tr>
<tr><td>What do we</td><td>make of it?</td></tr>
</table>

MY MAYA

> *"…some of the last inscriptions are gibberish, as if scribes had
> lost the knowledge of writing and were reduced to meaningless
> imitation of their ancestors."*
>
> CHARLES MANN 1491

no one who saw	*rat tat*	we copy shapes
the jaguar move	*hammer tap*	from the past
is left to say	*chisels awls*	
if his tail	*still life*	before city squares
(always this yellow)	*in tools*	parsed the jungle
curled this way		
nowadays	chips slip	*signs*
chisels are fine	into script	*without*
so thin the lines	high art	*vision*
toothy gods	fits the	
or kings	g r i d	
fine feathered		
serpent wings		
back steles against	*cross hatch*	some gum hunter
the invading forest	*snake belly*	who tops trees
	tongue and beak	might dare say
	rodent bone	the quetzal never
	knife haft	perched this way
	ear lobe	
	an axe	

afterwards
cross   You have to
but the sky and the sands   nothing
but the bones   and   nothing
sounds,   of singing, sometimes of
wailing;
of spirits   another
visions of   illusions,
gleaming   and waving   constantly
shifting
calls   A voice behind
patter

A STUDY OF DUST AND FROGS

No amount of showering can remove
the dust I feel settling on me now
at the end of the work day.

A cloud of fine, dry particles,
regarded as the result of disintegration
or the substance of the grave.

I stand alone with the herd at the White Plains
station as dusk goes deeper and dark birds—
are they crows—sail over and under the branches

reminders of essential things
I thought had to happen but never did.

A dispirited friend says *I feel*
nonexistent. Like a frog.
But frogs exist, I say.

Confusion, agitation, commotion.
Dust settling and unsettling.

Frog, frogs, just the word or thought of them
makes something in me perk up
something green, moist, magical
(I wanted to say vaginal).

Remember the frog odes Galway played
to break fledgling poets into song?

Remember the frog friend I longed for
as a child, not a prince, but the real wet-lipped thing
crouching and attentive, croaking and singing?

And then (hard to say to anyone)
there was the frog that came to the door
the night my sister died.

O dusty precepts of a bygone era.

The memory of her is of mistake
layered on mistake: psychotic break,
Thorazine, accidental overdose
not realized until it was too late.

Her shining-in-advance-of-everything
apricot hair never to be seen again
though some autumn trees take up her color.

Ashes to ashes, dust to dust.

That night by the orange lamplight of a country kitchen
I saw the frog's live body spread out
across the glass outer door
as translucent and veined as an umbilical cord,
the inside of him not separated from the outside of him

my faintly brown little man
come to tell me everything
yes, before it was too late.

HARLEM LINES

I was riding a cement escalator above the ocean,
my hand talonlike on the rail,
cringing at the sight of that huge hospital
down there:
Earth.

I saw Highbridge Tower in the background,
the East River paralyzed, and the bridge at 132nd
diving in
head first.

~

All winter
the stream's black ink
wrote its way into the snow.

And I said to myself
So you think you're a wordsmith?
I'll polish your words
until you can see yourself in them.

Then a thought came to me:
we are ruled by miscellany.

~

There is an invisible nerve network out there
like secret writing it shows up when held
above the flame.

~

This is for the wacky conductor who told me
to look for dolphins in the Harlem.

~

Often the concept comes without the word.

~

The Wakefield owl I look for
every day on the west side of the train
is not an owl, not an eagle,
probably not even a peregrine falcon
but a red-tailed hawk.

~

My life's become the train
I can't remember my dreams:
In the morning, they're just
too feathery.

So I've taken interest in the plastic bags
caught by trees—their various
gestures, colors
always resemble something else.

~

The train takes a bold stroke
out over the ice-clumped river.
This week I will practice
how not-to-care.

Quick Lumber
Desabolladura Y Pintura

Well-wrought this wall: Weirds broke it.
The stronghold burst . . .

~

Hitherto
only
effigies

~

Effects (as in personal)
Things . . . the sad silly evidence of the things
as Shirley Hazzard says in *The Great Fire*

though, naturally, I'd prefer her other vein:
In those days, their bodies were taking
reciprocal shape, tentative, delectable.

~

Hitherto (the poems were)
only
effigies.

~

Gas Heats Best
freedom's in the air.
This hint of spring
is not *suggestion*.

~

The sweep of my life
keeps getting swept away.
So I have been dipping my hand
into death
like a bear
scooping at honey.

~

No Wakefield owl
today (or yesterday).

~

Goad—I look up the origin and come upon
spear, propel, prick

Tuck-It-Away.
Gentleman's Cabaret.
Go-Go Girls (the meaning depends on
whether you want to stress
one *go* or two).
Sin City.

~

Masculine—the word itself
has a certain odor
musk-ox-like
though perhaps
not as heavy
as it seems.

~

Very like a bird
these tree limbs' shadows
when they stir.

{ THE **COLOR** *they partake of* NOW }

THIEF

A side door unlatched, she enters, thought crossing
the mind.   Sings a string of words under her breath.   Forager.
In the study, mahogany roll-top desk, a framed topography of
the moon.   *Mare Marginis.*   A skein of geese skims the roof,
the honks may mean encouragement, or warning.   A series
of gentle tugs.   If it comes to it, decamp and let the Thracian
have your shield, Archilochos.   Hand reaches into pigeonholes,
rifles through cigar-box drawers: frayed postcards, tangled
filigree chain. Pulls open a tiny square door, a knob for a doll
to grasp.   Map of the wind road.   Unlockable.   Outside
you could have heard their wings flap.   Folds the chart
under her arm, a delusion to want to unravel it.

ODE TO BROWN

Every morning they are still there
flanking the tracks:

brown limbs of the stick figured trees
behind pin curls of barbed wire

pre- or post-figuring what?

~

The color they partake of now

> *Brown wanting to become gold*
> *but stuck in what it is*

goes with me into the gaze of
Dr. Cranendonk's radiating eyes
in the orgone therapy room years back.

> *Tiger eye. Tiger lily.*

Cranendonk, my gentle Thor,
six feet four with feet too long for shoes.

He'd been in the War,
the Underground,
and could say: *I was afraid.*

His large, warm hands
cradle my brain even now
when I think of him.

~

My express train flies through and past
the flit, glint, riff of life.
Nothing to hold on to.

*These limbed inhabitants of Earth are the place where nests appear
and blend in. This brown is the color that seems to be background for
something else until it alights like the goldfinch painted by Fabritius,
a bird yellow, ochre, and brown that appears to flick its plumage
within the small, still canvas. Fabritius died the same year he
painted the bird. Killed in the Delft Gunpowder Explosion in 1654.*

Note the brown noun-ness of the bare trees:
brown-gray-hideaway brown,
the color when the color in my hair begins to leave.

And the shadows of the trees
becoming more definite
than what they emanate from.

~

So how should I come at things?
With a slant or Eros's arrow?
Moot point as the arrow's already in

heart's lodge.
Hear the *dge dge* where the pain
meets the heart-thrump?

I swear I'll learn to swallow
my own tail,
be utterly economical.

MORNING PRAYER: RIVERDALE, JULY 2006

Saturday morning and the men
hurry to synagogue with their *tallit* bags,
I'm jogging past them

thinking about things the way you can
when you know your route,
a military maneuver,

played over in your mind's eye again and again
until all you're left with is the after-space,
your feet simply punctuation,

a line break
on the curve to nothing.
Pray for peace, that's it.

Pray like the squirrel in the grass
with a crab apple in his mouth,
gooseberries barely visible in the thicket,

starlings splashing in pot holes,
the old woman who walks with a cane
to the market for the morning paper,

yellow blossoms turning into tomatoes,
green globes, new planets waiting,
waiting to be named.

THE QUILTS OF GEE'S BEND, ALABAMA

Start at the center.
Don't worry.
Your idea of what you're about to do
is going to become something else.

The colors will stare out at you—
having their say
in their own
quirk-ridden way—

patterns next to solids—
fainting lavenders
jutting up against cooling limes—

dungaree blues of a dead lover—
neighboring more dungaree blue—
pliant cottons and unwieldy cords
that bunched up—
refusing to lie flat.

You are going to make something to cover yourself with—
something to keep the kids warm—
something to lie under
made out of the dead, loved, worn-out, used-up-entirely-
in-this-life.

Because nothing is ever wasted.
We had nothing to buy anything with.
Lives were so hard.
You wouldn't believe me if I told you
how hard our lives were.

The torn fabrics will come together—
orange against white against black—
a little bit of cherry on the lower left:

no neat flowers in the quilting—
no tiny orderly squares
when you stand back.

The thread will leap frog
wherever it wants to—
free to create arches and off-center webs:
star trails on which gazers can't help but stick.

MERCURY

I dreamt of fish.
They were small and I was letting them go,
pouring a bag into the pond.

Summer.
That slowness coming up
out of the sidewalk grass.

Jonas catches a dragonfly,
green legs and wings,
Mercury has no moon.

Cherries after my Aunt Gretel's funeral.
Juice ran down my chin.
My fingers are stained

red like meat my aunt
would hang in her butcher shop
on Columbus Avenue in 1972.

If someone stole a chicken
she ran after them.
And said, "If you really need it, take it.

But don't take without asking."
Gretel would tell this often,
gesturing with her large hands.

IMPRESSIONISM

I ride amid the
overwhelming ones—
airy bird songs
and swaying weeds

headlong into the field
of being itself

Because the dead
some of whom
I still love
live there—

perceived as fleeing
across this hayfield now

Leaving their willowy imprints
that let go their hold almost
as soon as they're made

Here and gone
here and gone
instantaneous
on the green

So when seen
from a distance
there is this slight
lag or lapse

between the impression
on the grass
and its release

which gives rise to a sheen
that moves
as if light and wind
were pigments mixed

Which is why
I said
willowy:

If you watch a willow
in the wind
you'll notice a half-beat

or more interval
between what
the willow limbs do

after what's done
to them
happens.

COURTSHIP'S A BORING *negotiation of* TERMS

It's true she is her father's
pet, but he's fierce
of temper and rash, at times,
with pride. And then

she is tired of her sisters,
bossy, with their lightweight
princes. To leave home,

she needs a husband, but
courtship's a boring

negotiation of terms. One day,

wild like her father,
she suddenly, stubbornly

refuses to speak—losing suitors,
family, dowry in one fell
swoop. *Nothing will come*

of nothing. Listen: no heath
roaming for this girl. *Most*
rich being poor, veracious
and voracious, she returns

to save, or try to save, the one
who banished her. *O, reason not*
the need. She comes to fight

her pelican sisters, neither forgot
nor forgiven. To fight, to feel

the dust the rough wind blows across her face.

They're gone now, so I can miss them,
decidedly dead. Even the latest bloomers

blighted— skeletal chrysanthemums
crackling in the wind, the last asters ashen.

Like a young wife pawed nightly
by an aging mate, clinging in smiles

to his arm, carrying on as if
it were the best of honeymoons,

that persistent green had begun
to look glazed, dazed, no longer engaged

against November's last bastion,
but papering over the catastrophe.

Saddest were the late buds,
their doomed blooms furled,

soon to be thoroughly browned,
sepia shadows of themselves.

Those who are inflexible, the Tao says,
are in harmony with dying.

Now I can miss them, wish them back
and forget the ghastly slowness of their going.

YOU

The water makes me think of you,
newspaper, salt, pepper,

wind through leaves,
rabbit by the bridge

balloons floating,
filled with breath.

The same questions
hover over us

as on the morning you said
yes even to the turtle

who came out of the marsh
and rested on our front lawn

head tucked in deep
shell warming with each passing minute.

Come lie next to me.

HUMBLE

The little dog loves the leash.
He's the cheerful child

of anyone who's got the latch
to attach to the halter on his back.

On our way, we're polite
at first—we pace carefully.

I allow him his ecstasies
around trees and odd debris

and he ends his enthusiasm
before he's quite done—

with Pomeranian courtesy
allowing me to be the one

in charge. Yet when his ardor
at the scent of a friend or cat

bores me, I will carry him off—
we both know that.

So why next time will he still
prance and curl

at the sound of his chain?

HITTING THE SIAMESE

Whose idea was it getting a cat?
The lady from the shelter had said it:
Siamese like to talk, talk, talk. She also checked
The windows for cat-proofing and advised
We shield the ficus with balloons. *Go scratch that!*
Yet what shot me out of bed that night near the end
Wasn't the "talk" or the hissed words we'd exchanged
But a string of baby-like bellows
With a slight rasp in the lower range.
What could he possibly want then—
More quality time with his estranged masters?
Locked out of the bedroom by 10 PM
So he wouldn't bite our ankles at 2 AM.
No—I blamed the short order cook whose kitchen
Faced our airtight ground floor apartment.
Kitty kitty, he'd sing out from his window, *Here kitty kitty,*
In an Aaron Neville falsetto.
And the dumb animal would sit behind the screen and wait
For his cue, the song, the call, a promise.
There never was a thing for kitty.
I suppose I could've asked the cook to stop.
Instead, that night,
I went and picked our cat
By the fixed fur of his hind
Where it would hurt more, yank followed by yelp.
The beast within released
He closed his striking blue eyes each time
I slapped his face like a lover's, a prisoner's, and growled,
Shut it, shut it, shut it, shut it!
Wanting a confession, an apology, a way to save our marriage.

EROTIC DREAMS

Mine are more emotional.
He's holding me in complete understanding,
my pleasures are his. All this happens

on a street corner. I've come home again.
His arms, a thought, tight—
the sensation a poem.
Earth is warm and wet

before dawn. His hands, profile,
eyelashes are lunar.
I am spilling over with
the opposite of loneliness.

What would that be in this full green hour?

AUTUMN REMONSTRATION

Couple-hungry, full-grown but still in your teens,
off limits and thus irresistible,
you tweak my demon urge. Rusty at first,
then all too lubricated, my sexed brain
banters with itself, is finally convinced
it is not you I want to fuck to quivering.
Myself? My own desire?
Lust, lust, love's my snare, the lure of the mind,
the wit of you, your words and photographs.

At first, what I fear is success, a succubus,
a love-pit soft and bottomless. You seem
so poised to fall, ripe boy. My mind plays films
sticky and raw—the young bridegroom smothering
in feathers plucked for his bed,
myself an ogre at the feast, gobbling
youth's wet rations.

                                        After a week apart,
I've tried to imagine you plain, even grotesque,
safely unappealing, safely young.
Face-to-face I find your features all too pleasing:
eyes the greener side of hazel,
a patch of hair above your t-shirt collar.

Because I am the wiser one, I know
the choice is mine to make—or so it seems.
I will not smooth your hair, still snarled from sleep;
I will not touch your knee by accident.
Above all, when you mention a girlfriend,
I will not let flat grief replace this tug.

I release rights to your wit, your sweat, your passion
for whatever nudes you shoot or words you write.
I will not let myself be gazed upon.
Young man crepuscular, you're on your own,
to find out what nights hold and days can hide.

{ THE **BODY**

gets farther AWAY }

LATER THE SAME DAY

In the distance of the afternoon she lies on a boulder
lodged in the stream. Bulwark. Crossed water-brushed stones
to reach it. What you may stumble over, fortuitous, earthly. Letters
forgotten in desk drawers.   Snow melt rushes downhill, tumbles
under bank-gripping roots, splits into two or three channels. Records
of events that may or may not have happened. Bare shadows on red
oak trunks. Maybe there are footprints in the snow mud by the door,
clues. Unfolding of the universe as one accident after another. The
light this time of year. A note in the margin that, belatedly, solves
the mystery. Trespassed. At the bottom, level ground, the current
is one current, the stream bends out of sight. She was never able to
read the map. The slip of things.

PRE-DAWN DARK

The body gets farther away.

And ego-bound, disappointing intelligence
is a brilliant fizzle
of a falling star.

Remember Dad's hand
clenched without rest
in the final year of his life?

I often find my own
in the same position—
fingers and palm concentrating.
Bearing down as much as any brain
on something
neither he nor I could
ever see.

AT 4 AM

And cursing—his socks soaked most of the urine
Of what, fear? But he was too busy aiming, missing.
There was a pause, or I think there was, a gray instant
When pulling down his shorts I brushed the brush-like pubes.
One hour later I'm helping him stay upright, hand on his back.
"Is the offspring of a bathtub and a toilet bowl…"
He's said before, "…the bidet?"
Its feeble tickle of a fountain dislodging, rinsing, draining
As I wring the sponge in a downward motion and then hold my breath.
I apply and re-apply it between his buttocks,
He jokes, "Where no one can see it,"
"I don't like this town," "Why bother cleaning down there."
We are alone in the bathroom, door opened a crack.
And myself, trying to show everybody I've got the bolas,
An intern to my own family,
IV vine slung over his right shoulder.

A PHYSICS

The form holds indefinitely
in my mind's eye.

As if a dream—the body bare before me,
a pale slice in the night, hair wet from swimming.

      To say I'm eager to see you again
      would be an understatement
      for I am thus seeing you all the time

the pastel nude wavers
against the summer dark
a shimmer of shins

      Got the jitters? Give up the coffee,
      toss those pills, sniff instead the clear air
      of life's little inconsistencies

            dipping to reach a low note

Clothed, the male exhibits a decidedly retro style

            down, then up again

Unclothed, the torso glows, buttered with sweat

You. . . are. . . the breathless hush—

a slim gold box of impulse
studded with tiger's eye

You. . . are. . . the promised kiss—

You are the tenor, the tenor of my times

You've reached critical age
no more years can be added
without your being chemically altered
what of integrity?
time begins to tell

Once more unto the—

hull breach!

into the—

excuse me, did you say?

No. No answer.

Answer!

DISCLAIMER

If you are reading this

it is due to an error,

an oversight, or some otherwise

unprecedented act on the part

of the Management.

        blame it on the Moon

Do not be alarmed if

you hear a voice you are not accustomed to,

        screams

or if mention is made of subjects

        embarrassing nipples

out of your ordinary purview,

        "those stubborn bloodstains"

or if unfamiliar territory is mapped

intricately and with candor.

        that Moon, she brings—

Comfort yourself with the fact that

        if not blood, then at least—

you will soon be returned

to your regularly scheduled programming,

        "sorry, sorry, sorry"

with the requisite words from Our Sponsor.

Unless, of course, you prefer

To follow me away to the roof

hair curled to frame the face

to watch the white disk turn two-thirds

Lillian Gish on film, 1915

mottled sepia, then charcoal, then black,

then shyly bare her sharp white face entire.

RESISTING METAPHOR

What if it's like a nap
that dulls—hands lower
book drops
huge breath—desired
for all the mind's protests

Just one more page

Yet like nothing
memory of snow drift or rose
removed by one errant cell
less than the peel from death's
littlest fingernail—who has no hands,

itself unlike anything else.

Five-sided stars deep in hollyhock
and harbor—cat's haunch
and leap like the grasshopper's—
electrons like planets—
fish scales on butterflies—

life's ideas bear repeating.

Death's got only one.

It's the found thing—finding's over.
Searching for an author
almost, almost—too far back
there

Nothing more to look for

FLUIDITY

Be patient with me, my love, as my body feels
the clutch and pinch of yours as if for the first time.
I mean *the* first time, half my life ago, when
my young lover refused to wait for younger me. Impatient,
he took his share. A curtain tore in my heart,
the beginning of our end. First love, first blood,
first feeling pain, then liking it. I grew to love the pain,
then I grew out of him. My body was a vessel, a temple,
and all that rot. Now it is a field well plowed, and the harvest
sleeps next door while we try the tillage again.

Has it ever been easy for me, the tumble down
that rabbit hole where mind takes body,
body takes heart, *blood* takes all, the winner?
I almost can't remember, for your whiskers start
and prick. And now the pain's so sharp
I wonder if I've bled. We hear a cry.
My breasts leak milk, love spilling on the sheets,
but not staining. Oh for true fluidity,
motion without jerking, breathing open-mouthed
without a catch, a scratch, a cough in the throat.

Be patient, I ask, help me flow *with* you—your voice
and hands—dispel sounds from above—below—
our son's bedroom. So much of it is in the brain,
I'm told, our largest sexual organ. "Sex" sounds so base,
but I've used "love" too many times already here,
and it's just a euphemism for this bawdy function—
an arm here, a leg there, parts tangling, probing, flinching,
everything too slippery or too parched to work smoothly.
If I expect too much, my dear, forgive me, for after all
this fracas is the prickling force, the source.

It's not good to look back, see
what happened to Mme Lot, to
Eurydice—it's not even good
to be looked back at.   Unalterable
outcome behind, unavoidable
end ahead. That leaves
the middle—each moment
the center of your life
the way each point's the center
of the universe. Here you are.

{ WHAT **SHAPES** *do you* BECOME ? }

FIELD NOTES: THE MORPHOGRAPHER

How did you learn?
My mother showed me.

What shapes do you become?
A type of bird, a type of cat. Occasionally
the wind.

Do you choose when, or does it just happen?
When I need to. Or want. But as children
we sometimes
slip, alter unexpectedly.

So, you select your shape purposefully?
My own purpose. Either from the center or to
the center.

Isn't there a big difference?
Yes, regarding inspiration. But both are spirals.

Is spiraling part of shifting?
In the sense of singing, like smoke.

*What's with all these **s**-es?*
There's spirit, also.

SCAR

How delicately it runs down
your sternum, this seam paler
than your pale skin, sign
that something within has
been repaired and healed over.

After they cut you open and sewed
you back together, I longed to hold you
but could only stroke your head,
cradle your hand. Your eyelids fluttered,
your face reddened in a scream silenced
by the tube pressed against your vocal cords.

"She's crying," the nurse told us. Your voice,
softer than most infants' to begin with,
was lost until you coughed up the tube
and they had to take it out, breaking
post-op protocol. *I must be heard,*
and so you were, returning from
the anesthetic haze, dazed by pain

and morphine for the pain. Next morning,
the white-shoed woman who shuffles in
to take your x-ray hums, not gospel
or "Amazing Grace," but "Que Sera, Sera"—
a mother telling her child *What will be, will be*—
not quite *All's well,* but close. Your cries get stronger,
I beg another morphine shot for you.

Third day, I can nurse again, mindful
of your mended-china ribcage. Tears
come with the milk, and these liquids
are all I have to give, O daughter,
tiny warrior, silver-scar-bearer,
nothing at all wrong with your great heart.

BARBARA & THE ANGEL

"I'd rather see you naked than see you dead," Julianne
Moore recalls in an interview with Barbara Walters
what her mother always told her. What's more
luminous than Julianne on this rainy day? Barbara truly
cares about Julianne's happiness, and the elation of her
statements is contagious, so keep watching.

She becomes emotional when talking about her
impending marriage or the birth of her son,
who can be sure.

Barbara's mind wanders off. She's pushing a shopping
cart through an aisle where oranges shine
as speed limit signs.

Imbued in green hues, her eyes
are a war correspondent's
emerging from some abysmal well.

The sound is muted. All disappears.
Julianne and Barbara, gone
by the discharge of the remote.

In the darkness Barbara interviews herself.
She brings up the dream she had last night:

"An angel came in and had his way with my roommates
and my pet constrictor. There were fluids all over my
mortgage invoices even though I rent. My autographed
Che Guevara books, violated. By the way, what is it
with Che? He won't return e-mails or phone calls. He's
dead, isn't he"

Barbara goes on, "Why does nightime hurt so much?"
"Daytime is much worse," Julianne coos.

A drunk on the street
bangs on the stage door demanding
to hear the rest of the angel dream,
Barbara's saddest show ever.

"The angel was wearing a thrift store T-shirt," Barbara
continues. "Screens on my wall displayed a montage of
nude male bodies over images of dead soldiers. Outside
a caravan of army trucks idled in the green-hued night.
A flare opened up like a frigid sun while planes crossed
it as if mounted on wires…"

The angel lies next to her still,
a limb torn. No blood.
"Love love wake up."

"I'd rather see myself
interviewed than dead,"
the angel exhales.

THE MELANCHOLY BEAST

When the happy guy in me packs
His trapeze and tights

To move on to another town
This creature stays put.

Wild yet studied
He claws into my body

With the dexterity
Of a well-toned myth.

Once inside he fits my face over
His grim likeness.

As we sit in our corner
We become so stone-faced

Our collective chin drops
To my open chest

As if pushed off the lip
Of a bluff—

Watch the Sphinx shed
A weird, hefty tear

In front of an audience
Of astonished sand.

TERRAPIN

Easy to harvest as rocks, they kept alive on their backs,
so when the chickens drowned and the sheep died of fright,
the crew would still have fresh meat.

Now they'd been in the hold since Galapágos,
wedged against the bulkhead, a wall of upside-down domes.
The cabin boy went down to watch the massive feet

gesture out, waver, sense nothing and retreat.
He thought of future soup tureens, ladies' combs—
of one miraculously turned right, him on its back

trundling up and down between the casks—
of a reef that gashed a side deep enough to make a rift,
and he would ride away from the sinking ship—

Bad luck! he cried aloud, bracing against the hull,
fearful of his own mind, a trapped animal.

CHARCOAL

Find a place where your line
wants to take a journey,

    where the leaf pushes
    up against the window,

some curve in any direction
in the moment after sex

    before the air around you settles
    and the language names,

a place where skin meets light,
meets shadow, mother's mouth,

    young, in the camera
    as if she knew what you would become.

Let your hand tell you—
begin there, on the boat,

    the woman leaning over the deck,
    looking.

SAINT NOBODY

1

After great snow, the sun stings my window,
mad god who frightened infant Blake.
Random aches—first sign, no doubt, of some rare
terminal disease—make me wish I had no body
at all
                    I ain't got nobody
                    nobody
                    nobody

Lately the pain is sharpest where my wings would be.

Some days I'm like the Nobody
in *Goodnight Moon*:

Goodnight comb
Goodnight brush
Goodnight Nobody
Goodnight mush

Others, I'm Nobomommy to Blake's Nobodaddy—
that raggedy god always spouting No—No—No—
sporting the holy fool's cap and bells.

2

Nobody's Catechism:

Do you believe life is supposed to be less difficult than it is?
Once I believed, but now my eyes are open.

What now do you believe?
Life is difficult, because it is difficult.

Do you really believe life is what it is?
It's difficult to say.

Nobody's Communion:

Take and eat, this is my body
We eat until no body is left.

A mother is her own body feeding, bleeding

> *When somethin' is wrong with my baby*
> *Somethin' is wrong with me*

The baby is wrong—the wrong baby—who?
Nobaby. No, Baby.

3

She chose you, the midwife told us.
But the choice was ours.

I have to know, I'd terminate—I couldn't handle it.
I could've had the test, we could've known,
but we chose ignorance, had faith.

These children are God's special angels.
That's wrong, as wrong as Luther was
to call an idiot farm boy *changeling,*
order him drowned. The local prince refused.
Luther bade the people pray to be delivered
from this *devil,* who died within the year.

4

The word *retarded*, tossed from a dear friend's mouth,
feels sharp as swords or stones. I am no saint.

I don't know how you do it.
How? I don't.

Ah, vestigial angel-parts ache to emerge.

Nobody's Proverb:

It is better to be Nobody, white
figure in a cold upstairs window,
than the bearer of an errant womb.

   persona non grata, errata

Who's there?
Nobody here but us—
Nobody.

ACKNOWLEDGMENTS AND NOTES

GUILLERMO CASTRO

"A Good Word Like That," *EOAGH # 3*
"Barbara And The Angel" and "At 4 AM," *The Recluse*
"The Melancholy Beast," *Nth Position*

AMY LEMMON

"Karyotype," *Barrow Street* and
    The Center for Book Arts Broadside Series
"Autumn Remonstration," *Cincinnati Review*
"A Physics," *Los Angeles Review*
"Monday Aubade," *Poems and Plays*
"Disclaimer," "Saint Nobody," "Scar," *Prairie Schooner*
"Fluidity," *Rattapallax*

KATRINKA MOORE

"Cross- ing" and "Later the same day," *listenlight*
"Field Notes: the Morphographer,"
"Someone had marked on the page," and "Thief," *Otoliths*
"*A chance to redeem all sorrows,*" *Georgetown Review*

JOAN LAURI POOLE

"Azzurro", "The Quilts of Gee's Bend, Alabama," and
"Clear Night Outside Rite-Aid with Jupiter Overhead"
the Pearson Art Gallery's group shows
"Harlem Lines" borrows words from *The Great Fire* by
Shirley Hazzard, New York: Farrar, Straus, and Giroux,
2003; and from "The Ruin," *The Earliest English Poems*,
translated by Michael Alexander, Middlesex, England:
Penguin Classics, 1966.

"Ode to Brown" is for John Cranendonk

GUILLERMO CASTRO is a poet and translator. His work appears in *N^th Position, EOAGH, The Recluse, Bloom, Barrow Street, Lapetitezine, Frigatezine, Margin*, among others, and in the anthologies *Saints of Hysteria, This New Breed, Short Fuse, Poetry Nation*, and more. His translations of Olga Orozco, in collaboration with Ron Drummond, are featured in *Guernica, Terra Incognita, Visions*, and the *U.S. Latino Review*. He's also collaborated in a musical with composer Doug Geers, *How I Learned to Draw a Sheep*, providing the book and lyrics. Castro is the author of the chapbook *Toy Storm*. He lives in Astoria, Queens.

AMY LEMMON is the author of the poetry collections *Fine Motor* (Sow's Ear Poetry Review Press, 2008) and *Saint Nobody* (Red Hen Press, 2009). Her poems and essays have appeared in *Rolling Stone, New Letters, Prairie Schooner, Verse, Court Green, Barrow Street*, and many other magazines and anthologies. A Pushcart nominee, she is poetry editor of the online literary magazine *Ducts.org*. Selections from *ABBA: The Poems*, a sequence written in collaboration with Denise Duhamel, appear in several literary magazines and online at *Lafovea.org*. Amy holds a PhD in English/ Creative Writing from the University of Cincinnati and is the recipient of scholarships from the Vermont Studio Center, Sewanee Writers' Conference, West Chester Poetry Conference, and Antioch Writers' Workshop. She is an Associate Professor of English at the Fashion Institute of Technology in Manhattan and lives in Astoria, Queens.

KATRINKA MOORE won the New Women's Voices Prize in Poetry for her chapbook *This is Not a Story* (Finishing Line Press, 2003). "Restless" was nominated for a Pushcart Prize. Her poems have appeared in numerous magazines and anthologies, including *di-vêrse-city, The Little Magazine, Brooklyn Review, Poetry Motel, No Roses Review, Earth's Daughters*, and Milkweed Editions' *Stories from Where We Live: The Gulf Coast*.

JOAN LAURI POOLE lives in New York City and grew up on Manhattan's Upper West Side. Her poetry and prose have appeared in *Shenandoah, Mudfish, Mississippi Review, New York Quarterly*, and *Sculpture Review*, among other small magazines. She works in publishing and has also taught poetry workshops to undergraduates and elders. Her first book of poems, *My Bed of Crimson Joy*, is forthcoming from Carry Tiger Press. She holds a master's degree in English/ Creative Writing from New York University and has been a fellow at the MacDowell Colony and the Edward Albee "Barn."

ELIZABETH POREBA has been a high school English teacher for almost thirty years, and currently teaches at Bard High School Early College. She has two grown daughters, one of whom is a poet in her own right. She lives in Manhattan with her husband. She has published in *Southern Poetry Review, Poetry East*, and *Commonweal*.

SARAH STERN won both the 2005 and 2002 Bronx Recognizes Its Own (BRIO) Award for Excellence in Poetry. She was also awarded an Honorable Mention from the 2006 Anna Davidson Rosenberg Awards for Poems on the Jewish Experience, and a second Honorable Mention from *Lilith* Magazine's 2004 Charlotte Newberger Poetry Prize. Her poems have appeared in *The Mid-America Poetry Review, California Quarterly, Amelia, Parting Gifts, Treasure House, Bayou*, and various other publications. She is a press officer at The New School. She graduated from Barnard College and Columbia University's Graduate School of Journalism. She lives in the Bronx with her husband and two children.

www.ingramcontent.com/pod-product-compliance
Lightning Source LLC
Chambersburg PA
CBHW031320060726
47590CB00003B/1279